SPARKS OF LIFE

Chemical Elements that Make Life Possible

POTASSIUM

by

Jean F. Blashfield

RAINTREE
STECK-VAUGHN
PUBLISHERS

A Harcourt Company

Austin • New York
www.steck-vaughn.com

Special thanks to our technical consultant,
Philip T. Johns, Ph.D.
Associate Professor
University of Wisconsin–Whitewater

Development: Books Two, Delavan, Wisconsin
    Graphics: Krueger Graphics, Janesville, Wisconsin
    Interior Design: Peg Esposito
    Photo Research: Margie Benson
    Indexing: Winston E. Black

Raintree Steck-Vaughn Publisher's Staff:
    Publishing Director: Walter Kossmann   Project Editor: Sean Dolan
    Design Manager: Joyce Spicer   Electronic Production: Scott Melcer

Library of Congress Cataloging-in-Publication Data:
Blashfield, Jean F.
  Potassium / by Jean F. Blashfield.
    p. cm. — (Sparks of life)
  Includes bibliographical references and index.
  ISBN 0-7398-3451-7
    1. Potassium--Juvenile literature. 2. Potassium--Physiological aspects--Juvenile literature. [1. Potassium] I. Title.

  QD181.K1. B53 2001
  545'.383--dc21   00-045687

Printed and bound in the United States
1 2 3 4 5 6 7 8 9 LB 05 04 03 02 01

CONTENTS

K

Periodic Table of the Elements

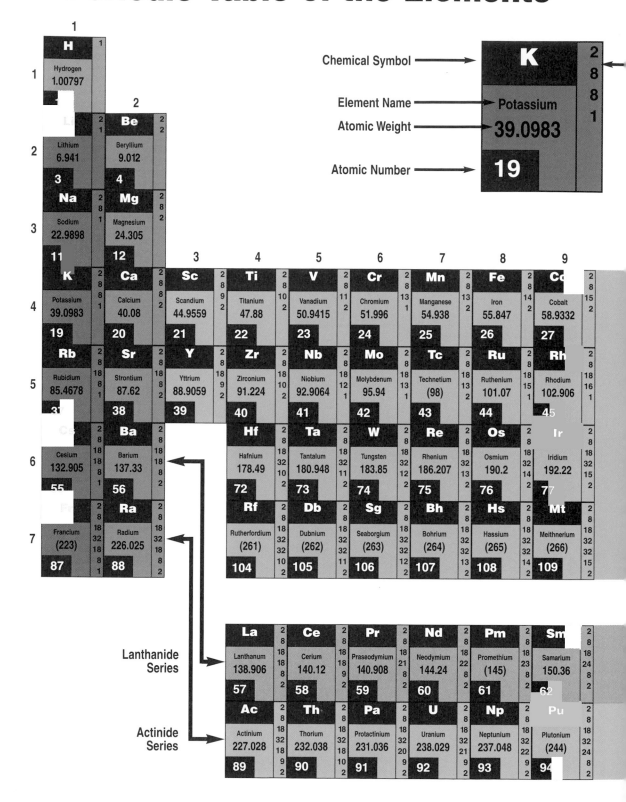

Chemical Symbol → K | 2 8 8 1

Element Name → Potassium

Atomic Weight → 39.0983

Atomic Number → 19

1								
H								
Hydrogen 1.00797								

2								
Be 2 2								
Beryllium 9.012								

	2 1 Lithium 6.941 / 3

Na 2 8 1	**Mg** 2 8 2
Sodium 22.9898 / 11	Magnesium 24.305 / 12

3	4	5	6	7	8	9
Sc 2 8 9 2 Scandium 44.9559 / 21	**Ti** 2 8 10 2 Titanium 47.88 / 22	**V** 2 8 11 2 Vanadium 50.9415 / 23	**Cr** 2 8 13 1 Chromium 51.996 / 24	**Mn** 2 8 13 2 Manganese 54.938 / 25	**Fe** 2 8 14 2 Iron 55.847 / 26	**Co** 2 8 15 2 Cobalt 58.9332 / 27

K 2 8 8 1 — Potassium 39.0983 / 19   **Ca** 2 8 8 2 — Calcium 40.08 / 20

Rb 2 8 18 8 1 Rubidium 85.4678 / 37	**Sr** 2 8 18 8 2 Strontium 87.62 / 38	**Y** 2 8 18 9 2 Yttrium 88.9059 / 39	**Zr** 2 8 18 10 2 Zirconium 91.224 / 40	**Nb** 2 8 18 12 1 Niobium 92.9064 / 41	**Mo** 2 8 18 13 1 Molybdenum 95.94 / 42	**Tc** 2 8 18 13 2 Technetium (98) / 43	**Ru** 2 8 18 15 1 Ruthenium 101.07 / 44	**Rh** 2 8 18 16 1 Rhodium 102.906 / 45

Cs 2 8 18 18 8 1 Cesium 132.905 / 55   **Ba** 2 8 18 18 8 2 Barium 137.33 / 56

Hf 2 8 18 32 10 2 Hafnium 178.49 / 72	**Ta** 2 8 18 32 11 2 Tantalum 180.948 / 73	**W** 2 8 18 32 12 2 Tungsten 183.85 / 74	**Re** 2 8 18 32 13 2 Rhenium 186.207 / 75	**Os** 2 8 18 32 14 2 Osmium 190.2 / 76	**Ir** 2 8 18 32 15 2 Iridium 192.22 / 77

Fr Francium (223) / 87   **Ra** 2 8 18 32 18 8 2 Radium 226.025 / 88

Rf 2 8 18 32 32 10 2 Rutherfordium (261) / 104	**Db** 2 8 18 32 32 11 2 Dubnium (262) / 105	**Sg** 2 8 18 32 32 12 2 Seaborgium (263) / 106	**Bh** 2 8 18 32 32 13 2 Bohrium (264) / 107	**Hs** 2 8 18 32 32 14 2 Hassium (265) / 108	**Mt** 2 8 18 32 32 15 2 Meithnerium (266) / 109

Lanthanide Series →

La 2 8 18 18 2 Lanthanum 138.906 / 57	**Ce** 2 8 18 18 2 Cerium 140.12 / 58	**Pr** 2 8 18 21 9 2 Praseodymium 140.908 / 59	**Nd** 2 8 18 22 8 2 Neodymium 144.24 / 60	**Pm** 2 8 18 23 8 2 Promethium (145) / 61	**Sm** 2 8 18 24 8 2 Samarium 150.36 / 62

Actinide Series →

Ac 2 8 18 32 18 9 2 Actinium 227.028 / 89	**Th** 2 8 18 32 18 10 2 Thorium 232.038 / 90	**Pa** 2 8 18 32 20 9 2 Protactinium 231.036 / 91	**U** 2 8 18 32 21 9 2 Uranium 238.029 / 92	**Np** 2 8 18 32 22 9 2 Neptunium 237.048 / 93	**Pu** 2 8 18 32 24 8 2 Plutonium (244) / 94

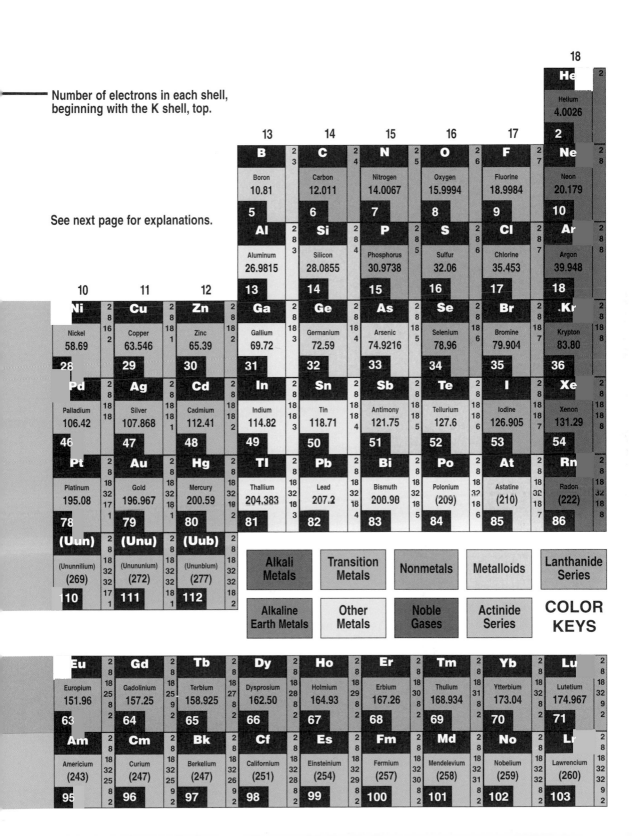

Number of electrons in each shell, beginning with the K shell, top.

See next page for explanations.

COLOR KEYS

Alkali Metals

Transition Metals

Nonmetals

Metalloids

Lanthanide Series

Alkaline Earth Metals

Other Metals

Noble Gases

Actinide Series

A Guide to the Periodic Table

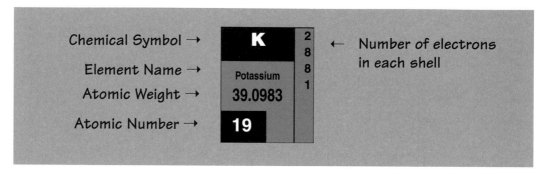

Chemical Symbol → **K**

Element Name → Potassium

Atomic Weight → **39.0983**

Atomic Number → **19**

2
8
8
1

← Number of electrons in each shell

Symbol = an abbreviation of an element name, agreed on by members of the International Union of Pure and Applied Chemistry. The idea to use symbols was started by a Swedish chemist, Jöns Jakob Berzelius, about 1814. Note that the elements with numbers 110, 111, and 112, which were "discovered" in 1996, have not yet been given official names.

Atomic number = the number of protons (particles with a positive electrical charge) in the nucleus of an atom of an element; also equal to the number of electrons (particles with a negative electrical charge) found in the shells, or rings, of an atom that does not have an electrical charge.

Atomic weight = the weight of an element compared to carbon. When the Periodic Table was first developed, hydrogen was used as the standard. It was given an atomic weight of 1, but that created some difficulties, and in 1962, the standard was changed to carbon-12, which is the most common form of the element carbon, with an atomic weight of 12.

The Periodic Table on pages 4 and 5 shows the atomic weight of carbon as 12.011 because an atomic weight is an average of the weights, or masses, of all the different naturally occurring forms of an atom. Each form, called an isotope, has a different number of neutrons (uncharged particles) in the nucleus. Most elements have several isotopes, but chemists assume that any two samples of an element are made up of the same mixture of isotopes and thus have the same mass, or weight.

Electron shells = regions surrounding the nucleus of an atom in which the electrons move. Historically, electron shells have been described as orbits similar to a planet's orbit. But actually they are whole areas of a specific energy level, in which certain electrons vibrate and move around. The shell closest to the nucleus, the K shell, can contain only 2 electrons. The K shell has the lowest energy level, and it is very hard to break its electrons away. The second shell, L, can contain only 8 electrons. Others may contain up to 32 electrons. The outer shell, in which chemical reactions occur, is called the valence shell.

Periods = horizontal rows of elements in the Periodic Table. A period contains all the elements with the same number of orbital shells of electrons. Note that the actinide and lanthanide (or rare earth) elements shown in rows below the main table really belong within the table, but it is not regarded as practical to print such a wide table as would be required.

Groups = vertical columns of elements in the Periodic Table; also called families. A group contains all elements that naturally have the same number of electrons in the outermost shell or orbital of the atom. Elements in a group tend to behave in similar ways.

Group 1 = alkali metals: very reactive and so never found in nature in their pure form. Bright, soft metals, they have one valence electron and, like all metals, conduct both electricity and heat.

Group 2 = alkaline earth metals: also very reactive and thus don't occur pure in nature. Harder and denser than alkali metals, they have two valence electrons that easily combine with other chemicals.

Groups 3–12 = transition metals: the great mass of metals, with a variable number of electrons; can exist in pure form.

Groups 13–17 = transition metals, metalloids, and nonmetals. Metalloids possess some characteristics of metals and some of nonmetals. Unlike metals and metalloids, nonmetals do not conduct electricity

Group 18 = noble, or rare, gases: in general, these nonmetallic gaseous elements do not react with other elements because their valence shells are full.

FROM THE ASHES

Long before chemistry became a science, discoveries were made about materials and their behavior. One of the substances that long fascinated experimenters was ashes left from wood fires. Somewhere along the line, someone discovered that if water were run through ashes and the mixture were boiled, a substance was formed that had a number of uses, such as in making glass and soap. The substance was given the name *potash* because it was prepared in a pot from ashes.

For a long time, the experimenters thought potash was a fundamental substance. Today, we know that potash is not fundamental—it is made up of the chemical elements potassium, carbon (symbol C, element #6), and oxygen (O, #8). An element is a substance that cannot be broken down further. Potash was sometimes called vegetable ash by early experimenters. They thought that another substance was the same thing. Of mineral origin, it was also called soda ash. Both substances were very caustic, meaning they could eat away, or corrode, materials. Most researchers thought soda ash and potash were the same, but British chemist Humphry Davy wasn't so certain.

Davy's Marvelous Machine

A self-educated scholar and poet, Davy was also a popular lecturer on science subjects. His major interests were electricity and chemistry. In 1794, an Italian named Alessandro Volta had invented a device that changed chemical energy into electrical energy. Called a battery, the device consisted of two different kinds of metal bars, called electrodes. One electrode attracted electrons and one gave out electrons. The two bars were submerged in a fluid called an electrolyte. The flow of electrons through the device was electricity.

Sir Humphry Davy

Davy knew that Volta's electrical device had recently been used to break apart, or decompose, water into its elements of oxygen and hydrogen (H, element #1). He hoped to use the same process, called electrolysis, to decompose other substances, especially the intriguing potash.

Davy constructed the largest battery made up to that time. He dissolved potash in a tank of water containing two metal bars as electrodes, with a battery in between. When the battery was connected between the metal bars, electricity began to flow through the solution. Suddenly droplets of a silvery metal began to collect on one bar.

Humphry Davy later determined that the metal could not be broken down further and must therefore be a new chemical element. He gave it the name *potassium* from "potash."

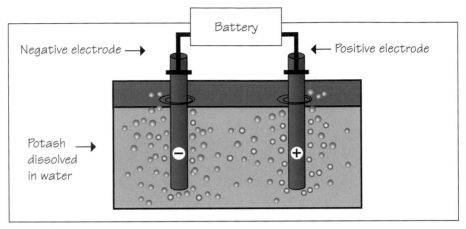

Humphry Davy's basic electrolysis apparatus, with which he discovered potassium and several other elements

The Twin Elements

The very next day, using the same equipment, Davy isolated another new element, sodium (Na, element #11). Then he knew that he had been right—soda ash and potash were two different substances. Potash came from plants and had potassium in it. Soda ash was a mineral and had sodium in it.

Potassium and sodium are very much alike. They exist in approximately the same amounts—they share the spotlight as the sixth and seventh most abundant elements on Earth. The only more abundant elements are oxygen, silicon (Si, element #14), aluminum (Al, #13), iron (Fe, #26), and calcium (Ca, #20).

When it comes to the ocean, though, there's a great deal more sodium than potassium. Both of these elements become part of seawater because they are dissolved from rock and carried by streams and rivers to the sea. But much of the potassium in fresh-water gets picked up by plants. As the sixth and seventh most abundant elements, potassium and sodium are about equal in amount. But they are in different places. Potassium is found mostly in living organisms, while sodium is mostly in the ocean, where it is tied up with chlorine (Cl, element #17) as sodium chloride, NaCl. This compound is better known as table salt.

K for Kali

Potassium might easily have been given the name *kalium,* from the Arabic word *kali,* used by Arab alchemists for the ashes of burned plants. Though Davy gave it a different name, it was given the atomic symbol K for *kalium.* Compound names that start with "kali" indicate that the substance contains potassium. For example, kaliborite is a mineral that contains both potassium and the element boron (B, element #5). The Arabic *kali* also gives us the word "alkali," as in the term "alkaline."

A silver-colored metal, potassium can be cut almost as easily as butter. It is the second softest metal. Only lithium (Li, element #3) is softer. When potassium is put into flame, the flame turns lavender in color. When it is evaporated, potassium's vapor is greenish.

Potassium has atomic number 19, meaning that there are 19 protons, which are positively charged particles, in the nucleus of a potassium atom. In the regions called orbits, or shells, around the nucleus, 19 electrons, or negatively charged particles, move. An atom with all its electrons is electrically neutral because the protons and electrons balance each other.

In addition to protons, the nucleus

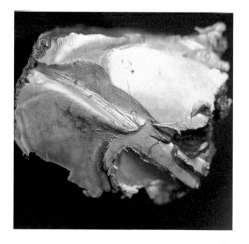

A chunk of pure potassium, a soft metal. It loses its shine immediately by reaction with the oxygen in air.

also contains neutrons, which have no electrical charge. The most common type of potassium atoms contains 20 neutrons, giving those atoms an atomic weight, or mass, of 39. However, there are other kinds of potassium atoms with different numbers of neutrons. Taken as an average, these different atoms of potassium give the element as a whole an atomic weight of 39.0983.

Potassium is in Group 1 (also called Group IA), the first column of the Periodic Table of the Elements. All the elements in Group I are called alkali metals because they form alkalis, or bases. Bases are slippery substances that are the chemical opposite of acids.

Chemists classify substances as acid or base (alkali) depending on how they react with the element hydrogen when dissolved in water. Hydrogen is the simplest element. Its atoms consist of only a positive proton and a negative electron, with a varying number of neutrons in the nucleus.

A hydrogen ion is one that has lost its single electron, leaving a positively charged nucleus, which is a proton. Bases, or alkalis, are substances that, when dissolved in water, take up these ions. They are the opposite of acids, which, when dissolved in water, release hydrogen ions. When acids and bases are mixed together, they can neutralize each other.

The other alkali metals in Group 1 are lithium, sodium, rubidium (Rb, element #37), cesium (Cs, #55), and francium (Fr, #87). (Note that though hydrogen is at the top of the column on page 4, it is there only because it's a convenient place to put it on the table. Hydrogen is not an alkali metal.)

Elements combine with other elements by sharing or giving up electrons. Atoms of alkali metals have only one electron in the outer region, or valence shell, in which electrons orbit the nucleus. These elements easily give up this lone electron, making them very reactive elements. Potassium may even explode.

When Davy separated potassium metal from potash, the

water around the silver droplets began to pop and fizz and form a lavender-colored flame. The single electrons in the outer shells of the potassium atoms were reacting with the oxygen in the water. The product of the colorful reaction was potassium oxide, K_2O.

Pure Potassium and Strange Oxides

Pure potassium cannot exist in nature in its free state because of that reactive lone electron. It is always found in compounds, which are substances made up of two or more elements. The main source of potassium used in manufacturing is potassium chloride, KCl.

When potassium metal is put into a flame, the flame turns lavender colored.

Pure potassium is obtained by reacting melted potassium chloride with sodium vapor, or gas, at a temperature of 870°C (1598°F). The sodium steals the chlorine from the potassium, forming a salt, sodium chloride:

$$Na + KCl \rightarrow K + NaCl$$

There's not much use for pure potassium, except in alloys (which are mixtures of metals, not compounds) with sodium. Such alloys are used in nuclear reactors.

It's a good thing there isn't much use for pure potassium because the pure silver-colored metal quickly oxidizes, changing color, when exposed to fairly dry air. It turns dark gray on the outside as the outer layer forms a coating of potassium oxide.

It takes two atoms of potassium to form a molecule with one atom of oxygen (whether from air or water) because oxygen has six electrons in its outer, or valence, shell. It wants to take on two more to complete that shell and become stable, or nonreacting. The potassium atom has only one electron in its valence shell. Therefore, one oxygen atom attaches itself to two potassium atoms, and they form potassium oxide, which is stable:

$$4K + O_2 \rightarrow 2K_2O$$

But if air around potassium metal has too much water vapor in it, something different happens. The molecules of water in the air combine with the potassium atoms to form both the compound potassium hydroxide and pure hydrogen gas.

$$2K + 2H_2O \rightarrow 2KOH + H_2$$

The heat given off as this reaction takes place ignites the hydrogen gas and the chemicals burn.

In extra-dry air (all normal air contains some water vapor), yet another reaction takes place. The potassium reacts with the oxygen alone to form an unusual molecule called potassium superoxide, KO_2.

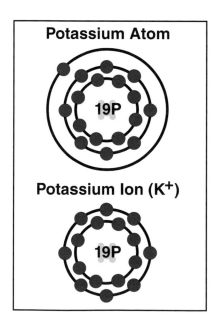

Potassium Atom

19P

Potassium Ion (K⁺)

19P

The Ion

Because potassium gives up its outer electron so easily, atoms of potassium are most likely to occur as ions. Ions are atoms that are missing one or more electrons or have an extra electron or two. In other words, they have an electrical charge.

The potassium ion is written K^+, which means that it is a positive ion—it has one more proton (a positive particle) in the nucleus than it has negative electrons in the shells around the nucleus. As we'll be seeing, potassium ions are of critical importance in living things.

ROCKS, ASHES, AND FERTILIZERS

For centuries, experimenters assumed that all potash had to come from the ash of burning plants. Then, in 1797, the German chemist Martin Klaproth found that the mineral called leucite contained potash. Leucite was found in Italy in places where lava from volcanoes had once flowed, especially near Mount Vesuvius. Farmers of the area knew that plants flourished when grown near that rock. They would break the rock up and add it to the soil in their fields to improve their crops. Even today, Italian farmers still use crushed leucite as a mineral potash fertilizer.

Scientists later found that potassium is a major element in many different kinds of rocks. It is found particularly in feldspars, which are aluminum and silicon rocks that originated inside the earth. Feldspars are the major

Muscovite is a mineral that contains a great deal of potassium.

component of igneous rocks, which were formed by molten rock that hardened. Orthoclase is a feldspar found in granite, which is often used as a building material. A rock called potash feldspar is a major ingredient in clays that are used in making china dishes and other ceramic products.

Samples of orthoclase feldspar, a potassium mineral found in granite rock

Micas are aluminum-based minerals that usually occur in flat sheets that are easily broken apart in layers. In many kinds of mica, potassium ions hold the layers of other atoms together. One kind of mica called muscovite has so much potassium that it is sometimes called potash mica. It is also called isinglass. Isinglass is so thin that it lets light through. Thin slices of isinglass were once used as windows in carriages.

Potassium-Argon Dating

There is so much potassium in rock that its abundance can be used as a way of dating rock. This technique is called potassium-argon dating. Argon (Ar, element #18) is an element that exists as a gas.

Most of the potassium in rock—93.3 percent of it—consists of the isotope K-39. The word *isotope* comes from Greek words meaning "same place." All forms of an element occupy the "same place" on the Periodic Table of the Elements. The nucleus of most potassium atoms is made up of 19 protons and 20 neutrons (19 + 20 = 39). However, there can be different numbers of neutrons and the element will still be potassium.

Potassium-40 is a natural radioactive isotope found in living things. Its nucleus contains 19 protons and 21 neutrons. This

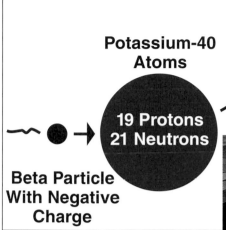

Potassium-40
Atoms

Argon-40
Atoms

18 Protons
22 Neutrons

19 Protons
21 Neutrons

Beta Particle
With Negative
Charge

Potassium-40 changes to argon-40 at a known rate. Scientists use special instruments to detect beta particles given off by rocks in which the change is occurring. The computer monitor at the left shows mineral particles in the rock sample being tested.

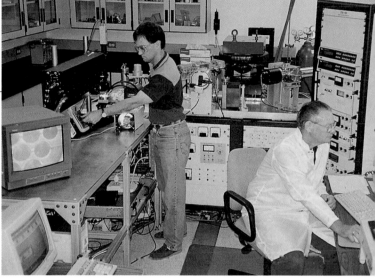

isotope has a half-life of more than 1.25 billion years. That means that it takes 1.25 billion years for half of the isotope to change, or decay, into other elements. Normally, 89 percent changes into calcium-40 and 11 percent into argon-40.

How do the atoms of one element change into atoms of a different element? The usual method is by natural bombardment of the atoms by particles from space. The solar wind, for example, is a stream of particles given off by the sun. One type of particle is called a beta particle. A beta particle, which may have a negative charge, can hit a proton in a potassium-40 nucleus, balancing its negative charge and making it neutral. A neutral particle in the nucleus is a neutron, not a proton, so the atom now has 18 protons and 22 neutrons. An element with 18 protons in the nucleus has atomic number 18. That element is argon.

The amount of K-40 and Ar-40 in a piece of rock, such as limestone, that was formed long ago can be measured. The proportion of the two isotopes can be calculated, giving an indication of the age of the rock. After this method of dating was discovered in 1938, certain rocks were found to be almost 4 billion years old.

The mineral sylvite has long been a source of potassium.

The Search for Potassium Sources

Plants require potassium, or potash, to grow properly. Farmers have known this for centuries. They tried to use sources that came from living things. For example, Indians of Peru in South America used guano, which was the dried droppings of seabirds that accumulated on rocks along the coast. For many decades, guano was mined like a mineral and shipped around the world, but then the supplies ran out.

Like the Italian farmers who used crushed leucite, other farmers tried to use rocks. Powdered granite is sometimes added to soil to provide potassium for plants. However, rock sources of potassium usually don't dissolve very well. The powdered rock may just sit in the soil, failing to provide the element the plants need. More useful ways of giving plants the elements they need were sought.

Immediately after the new United States government was formed in 1789, one of the first government offices set up was the U.S. Patent Office. The very first patent issued was to Samuel Hopkins of Vermont, on July 31, 1790. It was for a potassium, or potash, fertilizer.

The mineral called saltpeter, which is potassium nitrate, KNO_3, was first sought for its explosive use in gunpowder. It was later realized that saltpeter could be useful as a fertilizer because plants also need nitrogen (N, element #7). Saltpeter was found in deposits, usually where, in ancient times, water seeped down through limestone in the earth's crust. In the United States, the largest deposits were in the limestone cave area of Kentucky and southern Indiana.

The known potassium nitrate deposits were quickly used up for fertilizer. Fortunately, the mineral sylvite was identified in 1823. Like leucite, it was first identified on Mount Vesuvius in Italy. Sylvite is a rock made up of about 40 percent potassium chloride and nearly 60 percent sodium chloride.

Large deposits of sylvite were found in Stassfurt, Germany. Farmers in the United States used sylvite from Germany until it became unavailable during World War I. Geologists searched for deposits in the United States. They were found primarily at Searles Lake, California, and Carlsbad, New Mexico.

Searles Lake, an ancient dry lake bed in southern California, has been mined since the 1870s for its many different minerals. The two main potassium minerals in Searles Lake are sylvite and polyhalite, which contains a great deal of sulfur. The town of Trona grew up around Searles Lake to provide homes for workers who mine and process the minerals found there.

Canada has huge supplies of potassium chloride under the province of Saskatchewan where ancient marine deposits lie.

Heavy equipment is used to dig out huge quantities of potash in an underground mine in Canada.

There's probably enough potash there to last the world 600 years. However, the layer is not easy to reach because an ancient swamp of thick mud lies over it. Once reached, the layer is so thick that it has to be mined with heavy machinery.

Salt Sources

Today, the major sources of potassium are the mushy deposits called brine. These deposits originated when ancient seas evaporated, leaving behind huge quantities of the mineral salts that existed in the water. Potassium is the fourth most abundant element in seawater with about 380 parts per million (ppm).

Usually, water is pumped into the brine deposit, where it

dissolves the minerals and is pumped back to the surface. The water carries the minerals with it. There, two main potassium minerals—potassium chloride, KCl, and potassium sulfate, K_2SO_4—are separated out. (Sulfur is S, element #16.) In addition, considerable sodium chloride, NaCl, is obtained. Sodium is the second-most abundant mineral in seawater at 10,500 ppm.

The site of the ancient biblical cities of Sodom and Gomorrah is now the industrial town of Sedom in Israel. There, water is taken from the Dead Sea and processed for its mineral content. It is so filled with minerals that nothing can live in it, and it will keep people afloat with minimum effort. The water from the sea is evaporated to produce potash for use in fertilizer.

Once brine has been pumped from the ground into these settling ponds in Utah, the water content is allowed to evaporate. Left behind are mineral salts, especially potash.

POTASSIUM AND THE PLANT KINGDOM

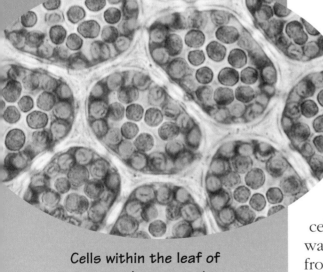

Cells within the leaf of a green plant contain chloroplasts (the small green round bodies), where photosynthesis takes place.

Plants create their own food from those nutrients that are present in the soil and air. Early researchers were certain that plants grew by actually taking part of the soil into themselves and turning it into leaves and stems. It was gradually discovered that, instead, plants make their own food through a complex, and quite amazing, process called photosynthesis, a word that literally means "putting together with light."

In photosynthesis, the plant's cells, in the presence of sunlight, use water and the nutrients that are drawn from the soil, plus carbon dioxide from the air, to create sugars and starches. As these substances are being produced, they store considerable energy, which will later be spent in performing the necessary acts of life, such as growing and reproducing.

Among the nutrients drawn in from soil are such elements as potassium. They are carried into the plant's cells in water, but they don't play a role in photosynthesis. Instead, they help to build plant structures. Potassium is used by the plant in strengthening cell walls. Strong cell walls allow plants to withstand greater extremes of heat and cold than they might otherwise be able to.

Flowing through a Plant

Plant cells, especially in the roots, have a characteristic called semipermeability. This means that water and the nutrients carried by water can go into the cells of the roots but can't go back out again. If cell walls were two-way streets, the plant couldn't stand or grow.

In any mixture of different liquids or gases, molecules making up the mixture have a tendency to spread out so that the different substances are equally concentrated throughout. This process is called diffusion.

Water enters the cells of the roots by diffusion because there is less water inside the cells than outside. It also moves up the special tissue of the stem called the xylem for the same reason—cells above have less water in them than cells below, so the water diffuses through the cell walls to equalize itself. The movement of water

Enlarged 1,000 times and given false colors, this photo of the xylem of a lettuce leaf shows the tube in which water moves upward by diffusion.

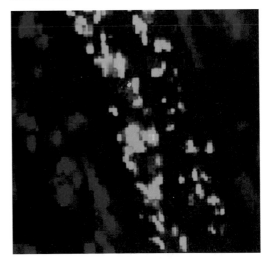

A deficiency of potassium is indicated by the yellow, curled edges of this leaf of a corn plant.

upward is triggered by the air and sunshine. These cause water to evaporate, or transpire, from tiny openings, called stomata, in the leaves. The sugars that are the product of photosynthesis move downward and outward as they are needed by different organs of the plant.

But what about the nutrients taken from the soil? In general, nutrients enter the plant as ions. The major chemicals in the soil are broken down into ions by being dissolved in water. Potassium exists as K^+ ions, the phosphorus (P, element #15) ions are hydrogen phosphate, HPO_4^{2-} (that means that the ion has two negative charges), and so on. These major nutrients are used by the plant for building structures and for critical chemical changes.

Ions do not move through the plant by diffusion, as water does. Instead, ions are actively pumped into the cells by the plant. The cells can keep admitting ions until the concentration is much higher inside the cell than outside. This situation would not happen if the ions moved strictly by diffusion.

Ions at Work

A huge amount of the potassium on Earth is bound up in plants, and yet the element doesn't take part in the physical structure of the plant. The actual function of the potassium within a plant has not been fully determined. It appears to play a role in the making and movement of carbohydrates and proteins within the plant.

It's easier to see what potassium does for a plant by the way the plant behaves when it doesn't have enough of the element. A plant that does not have enough potassium will reveal the deficiency by developing yellowed, often curling, edges on older leaves. On cereal grains, for example, the lower leaves look as if they were burned along the edges. On alfalfa, a cloverlike plant grown for animal feed, the leaves develop whitish spots.

The elements in soil interact with one another in providing the plant with what it needs. Too much of an element can interfere with a plant's ability to use other elements. For example, the more oxygen there is available in soil, the more readily plants absorb both potassium and phosphorus. Also, if a plant gets too much potassium, the excess can prevent the plant from using magnesium (Mg, element #12) properly, thus creating a deficiency in that nutrient. Potassium also plays a role in preventing plants from being harmed by too much nitrogen.

Dandelions thrive in soil with plenty of potassium.

Not all plants thrive on potassium. Dandelions do, but the people who are trying to achieve beautiful lawns don't want dandelions. However, they can plant a variety of grass seed that functions well without potassium ions. They will achieve two goals at once, having a nice green lawn, and *not* having dandelions.

Replenishing the Nutrients

Plants vary in how much potassium they take up from the soil. Alfalfa takes a great deal, which shows up in the meat we eat because cows eat alfalfa. Orchard trees take very little potassium out of the soil.

The supply of potassium in soil is limited. If it isn't replaced by a potassium-containing fertilizer, the more acid the soil becomes. This occurs because the potassium enters plant roots as a positive ion. The plant's chemistry determines that it is out of electrical balance and releases a hydronium ion (H_3O-) back out through the root tip to get back in balance. As hydronium ions accumulate, the soil becomes acidic. Many plants cannot thrive in soil that is too acidic.

Although most soils naturally contain a great deal of potassium, soils where crops have been grown over and over can become deficient in potassium content. It's been estimated that regularly used soil in the United States contains no more than 1 percent potassium, so it is vital for a good crop that the element be replaced regularly.

Today, fertilizers are available that can handle all sorts of plant needs. They can provide all the essential nutrients, as well as different percentages of the trace nutrients, such as iron and copper (Cu, element #29), that plants need in smaller amounts. The trace nutrients are *micro-nutrients*. Micronutrients are the elements needed in smaller quantities than macronutrients. Farmers and plant growers can pick out the nutrients they want.

On containers of fertilizers that are called complete, three numbers are given. They are in the order of N-P-K, nitrogen-phosphorus-potassium. The P content is in the form of any of several different phosphates. The K is usually in the form of

The figures on this bag of commercial garden fertilizer indicate that it contains 28 percent nitrogen and only 3 percent potassium and 3 percent phosphorus.

DO NOT USE ON ST. AUGUSTINEGRASS, FLORATAM, DICHONDRA, LIPPIA, CARPETGRASS OR BENTGRASS LAWNS

ACTIVE INGREDIENTS:
2,4-D† 1.21%
MCPP†† 1.21%
OTHER INGREDIENTS: 97.58%
EPA Reg. No. 538-28   Total 100.00%
EPA Est. No. 538-OH-1   †CAS #94-75-7 ††CAS #93-65-2
KEEP OUT OF REACH OF CHILDREN
CAUTION
See back for additional precautionary statements.

28-3-3
Made in U.S.A.
NET WEIGHT 14.29 lb (6.48 kg)

potassium chloride, KCl. The percentage of this compound contained in the fertilizer is slightly higher than the actual percentage of potassium by itself.

The N-P-K numbers don't add up to 100 percent of the ingredients in the fertilizer. There is usually quite a bit of inert—or nonreacting—material mixed in with the chemicals to make them easier to spread on fields.

Composting

The best way for soil to regain nutrients is by using the plants themselves. When plants die, they collapse into the soil, where bacteria decompose them back into their original nutrients. This natural recycling was the scheme devised by nature long ago, and it worked well, for the most part, until humans starting taking plants and using them far from where they grew.

Composting is the name given to returning natural plant and animal matter to the soil so that

Machines are used to turn the rows of compost material at a large composting operation.

the nutrients are restored to the soil in the way that nature did it before humans interfered. Individuals who garden gather leaves, chopped-up tree branches, grass trimmings, food waste (without meat), and perhaps some manure. They pile it in a place where not much air can get to the mixture. Large commercial and municipal composting operations let more air get to the composting material, but the process is slower.

A series of chemical reactions take place in the compost pile, creating heat and raising the temperature of the pile. Bacteria thrive in these conditions, and they gradually break down the material into an organic matter called humus. This can be stirred into soil, where it provides both moisture-holding ability and nutrients.

A skilled composter can make humus that contains specific nutrients. Various hays, such as soybean hay and alfalfa hay, or even salt-marsh hay, are useful to raise the level of potassium in compost. Banana skins are very high in potassium, as are cucumber and orange skins.

Eating plenty of fruits and vegetables guarantees considerable potassium in the diet. Strawberries (shown at right) are a good source of the element.

One potato can provide more than 700 milligrams of potassium, about one-third of a day's requirement.

Humus has a big advantage over artificial fertilizers in that the elements in humus are taken up slowly and are not easily washed away. A great deal of artificial fertilizer is largely wasted. Perhaps 20 percent of all potassium in artificial fertilizer is washed out—leached—by rain before the plants can absorb it.

Eating for Potassium

As they grow, certain plants—and certain plant parts—are better at accumulating potassium than others are. These foods make up an important part of our diets.

Seeds and nuts are particularly rich in potassium. Some of them consist of at least 1 percent potassium. Spinach is high in the element, as are oranges, melons, and bananas. Dried dates are among the highest potassium sources known. Potatoes are also high in potassium, but when they're served as french fries, the value of the nutrients they contain is negated by the fact that they are fried in fat.

Vegetarians—people who don't eat meat—tend to have more potassium in their bodies than meat-eaters do. In general, foods that have been processed a lot tend to be low in potassium. So, for example, fresh fruits and vegetables are better sources of this nutrient than frozen dinners.

ACTION IN THE LIVING CELL

The body of this man floating in the mineral-filled Dead Sea is made up of millions of cells that contain similar minerals.

The living human cell has been described as a little bag of potassium ions because there are so many of them and their jobs are so important. There are more potassium ions in the human body than any other electrolyte. The average adult body weighing about 155 pounds (70 kg) contains only about 4 ounces (113 grams) of potassium. Other animals have different amounts of potassium ions, but the basic jobs of these ions are about the same.

As Humphry Davy knew, potassium is an electrolyte, which is any substance that gives up or takes on electrons, and thus conducts electricity (which essentially is the flow of electrons). The important electrolytes in the human body are potassium, sodium, calcium, and chlorine. These are all ions, electrically charged atoms. Potassium, sodium, and calcium are in the form of positive ions, written K⁺, Na⁺, and Ca⁺. They have a positive charge because they have given up one electron in the case of potassium and sodium, and two electrons in the case of calcium. The chlorine ion, called chloride, is a negative ion, written Cl⁻.

Moving Fluids

Fluids, and the ions and compounds in fluids, move in and out of body cells all the time. This happens because, as we saw with plant cells, ions tend to move, or diffuse, into different areas until their concentrations are equal. But when a semipermeable membrane, such as one around a cell, is present, only the water moves through. The ions and bigger molecules can't move through the membrane to equalize the concentrations on both sides (except in special circumstances), so the water moves instead.

The flow of water through a semi-permeable membrane is called osmosis. It is a critical process in all the cells of the body.

Osmotic pressure is the force exerted on the semipermeable membrane by

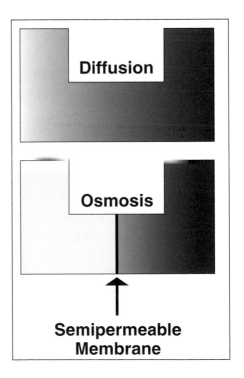

Diffusion

Osmosis

Semipermeable Membrane

Ions of two different substances tend to spread out evenly by the process of diffusion. A semipermeable cell membrane will keep the ions on one side and let only water through by osmosis.

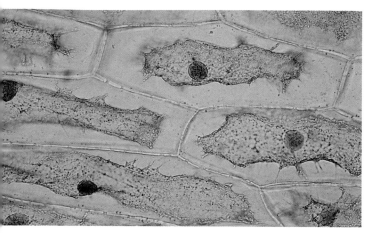

The interiors of plant cells are held within cell walls. In this photo of magnified onion cells, the cytoplasm (the material inside the living cell) has shrunk away from the cell walls because water has left the cells by osmosis.

the fluid on the side with a higher concentration of ions. This pressure is responsible for important fluid movement in the body. When ions are concentrated in body fluids outside the cells, water in the cells tends to go through the cell membranes in an attempt to equalize the pressure.

Pumping Potassium in Nerve Cells

Some processes, though, require that ions themselves move through cell membranes. One way that ions move through cell membranes involves the sodium-potassium pump. This pump is not a piece of high-tech equipment. It's the name biologists give to the mechanism in cell membranes that controls the chemicals that make nerves and muscles work. It controls the movement of sodium and potassium ions through the cell membranes.

A high concentration of potassium ions is needed inside the cells, but a high concentration of sodium ions is needed outside the cells. If diffusion were the only mechanism moving the ions, the two elements would be equal on each side of the cell wall. The sodium-potassium pump works against this tendency.

Potassium and sodium ions move during important body

processes. For example, a nerve sends a message to a muscle to contract. That message is sent in the form of electrical energy, specifically the movement of ions. Potassium ions leave the cells and sodium ions enter. Sodium-potassium pumps in the cells return the ions to where they belong so that they're in the right place the next time a nerve fires an impulse. For every three sodium molecules a pump moves out of a cell, it moves two potassium molecules in.

The pump is really a specialized molecule in the cell membrane. It attaches ions to itself and actively moves them across the membrane. The energy for the pump to work is provided by a chemical called ATP, or adenosine triphosphate.

Interestingly, the sodium-potassium pump does not work well at very cold temperatures. This might be the reason that people's fingers and toes ache in the cold. It is also the reason that human blood changes while being refrigerated to be given to somebody later. As it chills, the potassium ions leave the red

The sodium-potassium pump in a cell moves potassium ions out of the cell and sodium ions in.

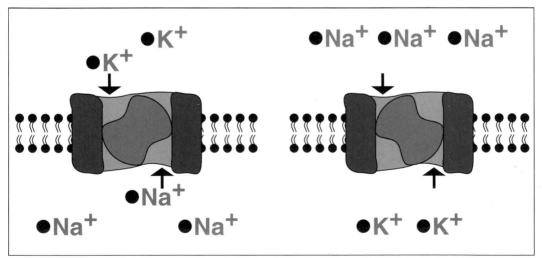

blood cells, where they are normally concentrated, and enter the blood fluid, or plasma. When the blood is warmed before use, the ions reenter the red blood cells.

Enzymes at Work

Enzymes are biological catalysts—substances that are necessary for a chemical reaction to take place but are not used up as a result of the reaction. Levels of potassium ions in the body fluids often serve as signals for various enzymes to do their jobs. One of the most important signals is in the ATP molecule.

In all living things, the ATP molecule is where energy is stored in cells—the energy to carry out the tasks of the cell. The ATP molecule temporarily splits to release its energy. The signal to split is an enzyme called sodium-potassium-activated ATPase (scientists add "ase" to the end of a chemical name to indicate that the chemical is an enzyme). This ATPase has been found to be the actual chemical—the "specialized molecule" mentioned above—that makes the sodium-potassium pump work.

A model of the ATP molecule. Energy is stored in the large phosphate ions attached at the far left. It is released by the action of potassium and sodium.

Pumping Action in the Heart

One of the most important places the sodium-potassium pump works is in the cells of the heart. Electrical signals make the heart work to pump blood. These signals occur because electrons can flow between the two different kinds of ions on the two sides of cell membranes.

When an electrical signal occurs in the heart, sodium ions enter a cell through a channel. The addition of the positive sodium ions changes the electrical balance in that cell. This change signals ions to go into the next cells, where the same thing happens. This progressive change in electrical conduction becomes a contraction of the heart muscle. A series of contractions moves blood through arteries and veins from the heart to the body and lungs and then back to the heart again. The movement of ions through cells is thus responsible for making the heart work and keeping us alive.

If this intricate sequence is disrupted—perhaps from age, drugs, or severe stress—the different contractions may fire out of sequence. This causes a scary condition called atrial fibrillation. The heart muscle is working hard, but it isn't accomplishing what it needs to because the sequence of contractions is wrong. Usually a quick electrical shock to the heart will set the sequence right again.

Blood Pressure

Blood pressure is the amount of force that blood pumped from the heart exerts against the walls of the blood vessels. Tiny muscles in those vessel walls contract or relax depending on many different conditions within the body. One of those conditions is the chemical makeup of the blood.

Our blood pressure goes up and down all the time. It's lower at night than during the day. It's higher if a person is bent in an awkward position instead of standing or sitting straight.

A medical condition called hypertension means that a person's blood pressure is too high for too long a time. Hypertension can lead to heart disease and the loss of blood supply to the brain, which is called a stroke. Unfortunately, a person can have hypertension and not even know it, which is why the disease is sometimes referred to as the "silent killer."

Blood pressure is tied to both sodium ions and potassium ions. Most people get more sodium chloride in their food than is

Hypertension, or high blood pressure (the numbers indicate a measurement of blood pressure), can lead to constriction of the blood vessels and an enlarged heart, as well as other problems.

good for them, either because it's in their processed foods or because they add table salt when eating. Doctors think the extra sodium can lead to hypertension. Probably just as harmful is the fact that the same people probably get too little potassium.

Researchers aren't really certain why—or even if—salt is really the bad guy. They just assume it is because in societies where salt isn't used much, people rarely seem to have high blood pressure. However, people in those same cultures generally get considerable potassium in their diets.

With high blood pressure, as well as edema, which is the swelling of body tissues from too much fluid, the heart has to work extra hard to move blood through the body. A person with these conditions is often given medicines called diuretics. Diuretics remove excess fluid from body tissues and make the person urinate. However, diuretics also tend to draw potassium out of the body, and this element must be replaced. Usually, eating one banana a day will replace the lost potassium.

There is growing evidence that blood pressure can be lowered by taking extra potassium. A study was made of people with high blood pressure. It was found that those who consumed the most potassium—about 4,300 milligrams a day—were one third less likely to have a stroke than those whose diet included the least potassium.

Many people believe in taking mineral supplements (tablets or liquids) in the hope that they will prevent or help treat certain conditions. However, a study conducted in Canada indicates that potassium is effective against stroke only when it is obtained through diet, not through supplements.

Potassium Ions in the Stomach

As soon as you take a bite of food, special glands in the mouth give off a fluid called saliva that begins the process of digestion. Saliva is filled with electrolytes, mostly sodium and chloride. It also contains potassium ions. When saliva is flowing freely (when your mouth "waters"), you may notice a slight metallic taste. That is the taste of potassium ions.

Saliva helps make food moist enough to swallow. When the food reaches the stomach, it encounters another pump, similar to the sodium-potassium pump. This cellular pump—called the potassium-ion pump—pulls potassium ions out of the stomach, or gastric, fluid and replaces them with hydrogen ions. The potassium returns along with chloride ions, which then react with the hydrogen to form hydrochloric acid, HCl.

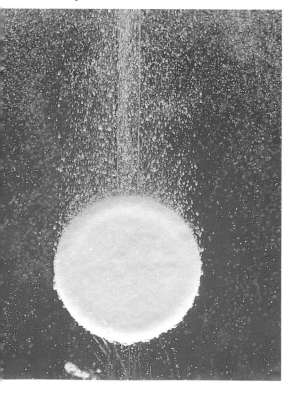

The fizzing of an antacid releases medicine to neutralize hydrochloric acid.

Hydrochloric acid is a very powerful acid, but it does not hurt the stomach because there is a thick layer of mucus inside the stomach that protects it. However, in some people, the acid backs up into the esophagus (the tube from the mouth into the stomach), causing a painful condition usually called heartburn, though it doesn't involve the heart.

Heartburn can be treated with a number of chemicals, most of them called antacids. One common antacid is potassium bicarbonate, $KHCO_3$, which neutralizes some of the hydrochloric acid in the stomach. It doesn't neutralize all the acid—no antacid does, because that would stop the functioning of the digestive processes, which require hydrochloric acid. Instead, an antacid neutralizes just enough of the acid to relieve the discomfort.

A newer treatment for heartburn is a medicine called cimetidine. It temporarily shuts down the mechanism of the potassium-ion pump in the stomach so that hydrochloric acid is not produced. The food that causes heartburn is out of the stomach and digested before acid is pumped again.

Storing Our Food

When we've eaten a big meal—perhaps lots of pasta, a salad, and a gooey dessert—we've ingested many of the substances called carbohydrates. The process of digestion breaks carbohydrates down into simple sugar, or glucose, $C_6H_{12}O_6$. Glucose is the form in which food is used in cells. It is "burned" (combined with oxygen), giving off heat energy in the process.

Plants made the sugar in the first place in the process of photosynthesis, but they assembled long chains of the sugar molecules into starches. Pasta is filled with starches.

Once our food is digested, about one-fourth of the glucose from that food is stored in the liver until it is distributed to the body cells. The remainder goes right to muscle cells, where it's stored until it's needed for a burst of energy.

Glucose is stored as a substance called glycogen, which is the same substance as starch in plants. When glucose is needed by the body, glycogen is broken down into glucose by enzymes. The same sodium-potassium pumps that move ions then transport the big sugar molecules into the body cells. There are also glucose pumps that move the molecules. Once in the cells, the glucose molecules are burned for energy, releasing water and carbon dioxide.

The process that began with plants taking carbon dioxide and water to make sugar, which stores energy, is just the reverse in humans. The cells in our bodies break down the sugars and give off carbon dioxide and water in the process. The cycle has been completed.

Sweating It Out

Sweating is a form of temperature control for the body in some mammals. When the temperature starts to rise internally, fluid leaves the body through tiny sweat glands in the skin. When the fluid, which is mostly water, evaporates, it carries some of the heat away with it.

Sweat glands secrete a solution of the ions of inorganic elements in the body, including potassium, chloride, and sodium, plus some other organic compounds. This fluid itself has no odor. The odor comes from the action of skin bacteria on the fluid as it sits on the skin.

Yes, exercise is good for you, but it's easy to sweat so much that you lose too much potassium. Athletes and people who work out every day should make certain that they get lots of potassium. Some so-called sports drinks, which contain electrolytes, can replace potassium ions. However, the more often you exercise, the fewer ions your body gives up when you sweat. Apparently, when it comes to exercise and sweat, "regular" is more important than "hard."

Too Much, Too Little

The body is not able to store potassium ions for future use, as it can some other ions. Therefore, lack of potassium in the blood occurs fairly frequently. There has to be a continuous supply of potassium in the foods we eat.

Sometimes a person can have so little potassium in the body that it leads to a condition called hypokalemia. This situation can result from malnutrition, diarrhea, vomiting, or the use of diuretics. Any of these can result in dehydration, or fluid loss. The excess fluid leaving the body carries too many K+ ions with it. These need to be replaced. A person who is seriously dehydrated, especially an infant or old person, may need to be

Heavy exercise has caused this athlete to sweat. Drinking a sports drink can replace the electrolytes that are lost through sweating, but be sure the label says it contains potassium ions.

hospitalized so that potassium and other vital electrolytes can be restored quickly and safely.

Hypokalemia makes a person feel generally ill and short of energy. The muscles may feel weak or sore and may cramp easily. If the situation isn't treated, perhaps by something as simple as eating bananas, veal, or broccoli, the heart may be affected, resulting in a weak pulse, dropping blood pressure, and finally heart failure.

Some researchers have proposed that there is a connection between the sometimes crippling joint inflammation disease called arthritis and a long-term deficiency of potassium. However, no major scientific studies have provided evidence that this is true.

The opposite situation—hyperkalemia, or too much potassium—can occur after an injury that crushes the body or severe burns, or if the kidneys are failing. The symptoms are actually very much like hypokalemia: a generally ill feeling, weakness, eventual heart involvement, with the added sign of mental confusion. Excess K^+ ions can build up in the body fluids. A blood test may show that the kidneys are not working properly.

The nervous system can also be harmed by an excess of potassium. K+ ions, which must be free to flow through cell-membrane channels, may become trapped within the cells if there is too much potassium in the fluid on the other side of the cell wall. The nerves fail to transmit electrical impulses. A sudden massive increase in the level of potassium in the body can be dangerous, primarily because of the effect on the transmission of nerve impulses.

Balancing Ions

For good health, it's not enough just to get lots of potassium from the foods you eat. The amount also has to be in the proper balance with the amount of sodium you get. A person who gets lots of sodium, perhaps from using too much table salt, and not enough potassium is vulnerable to high blood pressure, heart problems, strokes, and possibly even the development of cancer. All those potential problems can be helped by getting much more potassium than sodium. Lots of fresh fruits and vegetables and avoiding processed foods will do the trick.

People with hypertension are often told to switch to potassium chloride, KCl, to season their food instead of using sodium chloride, NaCl. Though it adds flavor to the food, too much potassium chloride can cause an irregular heartbeat. Also, it has a bitter aftertaste that sodium chloride doesn't. Other ingredients are usually added to mask the aftertaste.

Clearly, potassium plays a critical role in many processes of our bodies. We need as much of the element as we can get in our food in order for our bodies to keep functioning properly. A good amount to try for is 3,500 milligrams a day. Since almost all foods have some potassium, you can get 1,000 to 2,000 milligrams a day without even counting, but you'll need to concentrate on fruits and vegetables to reach the desired goal.

EXPLOSIONS, ELECTRICITY, AND THE ENVIRONMENT

Gunpowder, which contains potassium, was invented in ancient China and then introduced into Europe during the Middle Ages. Roger Bacon, an English scholar and monk in the thirteenth century, was the first person to write down the formula, although he probably got it from Arab alchemists. They were experimenters who believed that substances could be changed through a combination of chemistry, religion, and magic.

The potassium used in gunpowder was in the form of potassium nitrate, KNO_3, also called saltpeter. Other ingredients in gunpowder are carbon—in the form of charcoal from wood—and sulfur. Different amounts of

Potassium has been an important ingredient in fireworks since they were invented by the Chinese long ago.

43

these ingredients were used by different people through the ages, but the basic process remained the same.

When gunpowder is ignited, oxygen in the potassium nitrate feeds the explosive burning of the carbon and sulfur. If the chemicals are in an almost closed chamber, hot nitrogen gases rush out, propelling whatever might also be in the chamber, such as a cannonball or bullet.

The first known use of gunpowder—or black powder, as it was commonly called—in European warfare was in 1324. Iron balls were propelled at a stone wall a long distance away. The people defending the castle were stunned. The ability to shoot cannons and guns changed warfare forever.

Fireworks

Though black powder has been replaced by more modern nitrogen compounds in weapons, explosions involving potassium are still popular, especially on the Fourth of July. Potassium compounds are critical to fireworks because of the oxygen they contain.

Any fireworks that go off in the sky still use old-fashioned gunpowder to be sent aloft. Potassium nitrate is used with sulfur in fireworks displays to create white smoke.

Potassium chlorate, $KClO_3$, is also used in fireworks. It is used as the bursting charge in star-shaped fireworks. When $KClO_3$ is combined with salts of various elements, different colors can be created. Red color comes from strontium salts. Green comes from barium. Sodium produces a strong yellow color.

Potassium perchlorate, $KClO_4$, works with aluminum and sulfur to produce a big bang and a flash of light. It is a stronger oxidizer than potassium chlorate.

Potassium ferrocyanide is a yellow crystal used in manufacturing fireworks. The closely related potassium ferricyanide (which has one less potassium atom in the molecule) is one of the chemicals inside a light stick, which makes "cold light." Bending a light stick makes two chemicals inside it mix, creating light. Light sticks are popular with Halloween trick-or-treaters.

Making Electricity

Electricity is a form of energy derived from the flow of electrons, the negative particles in orbit around the nucleus of atoms. Electron flow exists as a fundamental aspect of natural materials, but the electricity we use in daily life keeps the electron flow within wires that direct the flow to where it is needed.

A battery contains chemicals that cause electrons to flow. One type is called an alkaline dry cell. The original batteries, like Humphry Davy's, contained a liquid as the electrolyte. A dry cell isn't really dry, but the chemicals are contained in a semisolid material instead of being liquid.

An alkaline dry cell has a casing of zinc (Zn, element #30) as the negative terminal, or anode, which gives up electrons. They move through a circuit to the positive cathode, where the material needs to acquire electrons to be electrically balanced. A light, radio, or other device lies between the two terminals so that the flow of electrons does work as it passes through.

The electrons making up the flow of electricity come from the electrolyte, which is a paste of

Structure of an alkaline dry cell

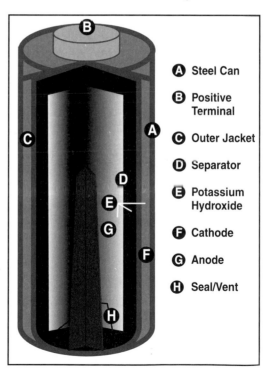

- **A** Steel Can
- **B** Positive Terminal
- **C** Outer Jacket
- **D** Separator
- **E** Potassium Hydroxide
- **F** Cathode
- **G** Anode
- **H** Seal/Vent

potassium hydroxide, KOH, called caustic potash. It is easily ionized into K^+ and OH^- ions.

An alkaline battery is more powerful than a nonalkaline flashlight battery. It can be used to produce electricity for a camera flash or to make larger toys move. These activities require more power than a flashlight does.

Fuel Cells

In a battery, the material making up the terminals, or electrodes, is gradually used up and the battery becomes useless. A device called a fuel cell is continuously fed new chemicals and thus can produce a continuous supply of electricity. One type developed for the space program was the alkaline fuel cell. It uses potassium hydroxide as the source of hydrogen to combine with oxygen from another source.

Potassium hydroxide is very corrosive, and not many materials can withstand the chemical for very long. The weight of the material needed to make a KOH fuel cell is too great for use in automobiles. But the search for a good replacement goes on so that cars can run efficiently on electricity instead of gasoline.

The KOH Molecule

For centuries, people have carried out a chemical reaction—whether they realized it or not—in the making of soap. Soap is a chemical product, made by heating a fat with a strong base, or alkali, such as potash. In the past, soap was made by cooking animal fat with wood ashes. The two heated ingredients would combine and harden into a clump of soap that could be used for washing clothing.

The most common soaps today are made from sodium hydroxide, NaOH, as the base. Potassium soaps are made with potassium hydroxide, KOH. Potassium soaps are generally softer than sodium soaps.

Because of this same facility for reacting with fat, potassium hydroxide is used as a drain cleaner. Clogs are usually formed around grease that failed to go down the drain. By very carefully pouring potassium hydroxide down a drain, you get the clog to turn into a soap that dissolves, unblocking the drain. Potassium hydroxide is one of the most corrosive common alkalis. It can burn the skin if handled improperly.

Potassium Chloride and the Environment

Potassium chloride, which can be a substitute for table salt in food, can also be a substitute for sodium chloride to melt ice on the streets of cities in winter. When a salt is dissolved in water, as it is when KCl is put on ice, it lowers the freezing point of the water and melts the ice. Potassium chloride is less harmful to the environment than sodium chloride, which can damage grasses and trees growing alongside the road, as well as make the metal on cars corrode.

Potassium chloride has another interesting environmental use. Water in clouds needs to gather around tiny solid particles

Potassium chloride, KCl, crystals. Their many uses include substituting for the more harmful sodium chloride crystals.

in order for raindrops to form and fall. It has been found that certain chemicals dropped into extra-cold clouds—a process called cloud seeding—may start raindrops forming. The first chemicals used were crystals of dry ice (carbon dioxide, CO_2) and silver iodide, AgI (iodine is I, element #53). Recently, the National Center for Atmospheric Research showed that a smoke of potassium chloride injected into a cloud can cause rain to form.

Salt from the Sea

Some people who live far from any ocean—in the Midwest, for example—may not get enough of the necessary element iodine in their diets. Iodine is a trace element, or micronutrient. It is needed by the body in only a tiny amount, but that amount is vital. Inadequate iodine can lead to a serious disease of the thyroid gland called goiter, which used to be very common. Iodine deficiency also shows as chronic fatigue and weight gain.

Today, the compound potassium iodide, KI, is added to most table salt sold in the United States to prevent thyroid problems. It doesn't take very much of the compound to keep a person healthy—1 part KI to 5,000 parts NaCl.

Potassium iodide is a salt itself. It's the product of the reaction of the acid hydrogen iodide, HI, with the base potassium hydroxide, KOH.

Super Breathing

Oxygen in the air exists as a diatomic element. That means that it joins two oxygen atoms together to make one stable molecule. When most elements are oxidized, they react with just one atom of oxygen at a time. Water, for example, is H_2O; carbon monoxide is CO.

Atoms of potassium and other alkali metals react with the oxygen in air so rapidly that they can attach themselves to both the atoms in the diatomic oxygen. This makes KO_2, which is

A scuba diver using an apparatus that makes potassium superoxide can stay down longer than one using a standard tank of compressed oxygen.

called potassium superoxide (regular potassium oxide is K_2O, also called potassium dioxide).

The superoxide is used in the breathing mechanism of scuba (*S*elf-*C*ontained *U*nderwater *B*reathing *A*pparatus) equipment. Regular scuba equipment includes a tank of compressed oxygen that is breathed in until the oxygen is used up. But potassium superoxide reacts with the carbon dioxide in the breath exhaled to produce more oxygen for breathing. The reaction is:

$$4KO_2 + 2CO_2 \rightarrow 2K_2CO_3 + 3O_2$$

potassium superoxide + carbon dioxide
$\rightarrow$ potassium carbonate + oxygen

Divers using superoxide equipment can stay underwater much longer than divers using traditional equipment.

A
POTASSIUM
CATALOG

The KREEPy Moon

Potassium is the K in the group of elements on the moon that have come to be called KREEP, for *K,* the symbol for potassium, *R*are-*E*arth *E*lements, and *P*hosphorus. "Rare earths" (which aren't really rare but were thought to be when they were discovered) is the name given long ago to the elements that make up Group 3 in the Periodic Table of the Elements. Other elements in the group include scandium (Sc, element #21), yttrium (Y, #39), and the lanthanide series (elements #57 through 71), which are shown in a separate row in the table on pages 4 and 5.

It has been determined by moon-orbiting spacecraft that KREEP is located primarily in *Mare Imbrium*, or the "Sea of

Astronaut James Irwin of Apollo 15 dug up lunar soil to take back to Earth for study.

Rains." That is the big, flat area where the Apollo 15 astronauts landed in 1971. It formed about 4.5 billion years ago. The KREEP in the flat area is apparently the last remnant of the moon's early history of being flooded by molten lava.

In the late 1990s, instruments aboard a spacecraft called Lunar Prospector found a very thin atmosphere of potassium and sodium atoms around the moon. The same elements had been found around the planet Mercury in 1985, surprising scientists.

The Sweet Things in Life

While one potassium compound is used to make things salty (potassium chloride), another is used to make them sweet. A new artificial sweetener began to be used in the United States in 1998. Acesulfame potassium, called ace K, does not have any aftertaste as some artificial sweeteners do. Also, unlike the popular artificial sweetener aspartame, ace K can be used in baked goods. Ace K is sweeter than aspartame but not nearly as sweet as saccharin.

Despite the fact that potassium is part of its name, the amount of white crystals of ace K needed to sweeten a cup of coffee contains only 10 milligrams of potassium. That's less than 3 percent of the amount in a banana. Ace K is not digested. It leaves the body unchanged in urine. It is used primarily in the manufacture of diet soft drinks.

Chocolate K

Potassium and chocolate seem an odd mix, but the element (chocolate is *not* an element!) plays an important role in the manufacturing of chocolate from cocoa beans. Cocoa itself is fairly acid, and some chocolate products taste right with slight acidity.

Dutch chocolate, however, is basic, or alkaline. It is made alkaline by adding potassium carbonate, K_2CO_3, to the cocoa. Chocolate lovers will be glad to know that there's also lots of

The manufacture of some kinds of chocolate requires the use of potassium carbonate as an alkalizing agent.

potassium in the final chocolate product. One 4-ounce (113-gram) chocolate bar contains 420 milligrams of potassium, about the same as in a big glass of orange juice.

Safety Matches

Plain old matches can be struck anywhere. The head of the match bears a lump of a phosphorus compound containing a little bit of potassium chlorate, $KClO_3$. It releases oxygen to support a flame when the head of the match is ignited by friction. Safety matches, however, keep the two compounds apart until a match is struck. The potassium chlorate and some other chemicals are on the match head, while the phosphorus is mixed with a rough, sandy material on the striking surface of the box.

The Laser Tattoo Remover

Different kinds of lasers do different kinds of work on human beings, because the concentrated light rays they give off are attracted to different kinds of tissue. The KTP laser (KTP stands for potassium-titanyl-phosphate)—produces wavelengths of radiation that can be absorbed by molecules in the skin. The rays a

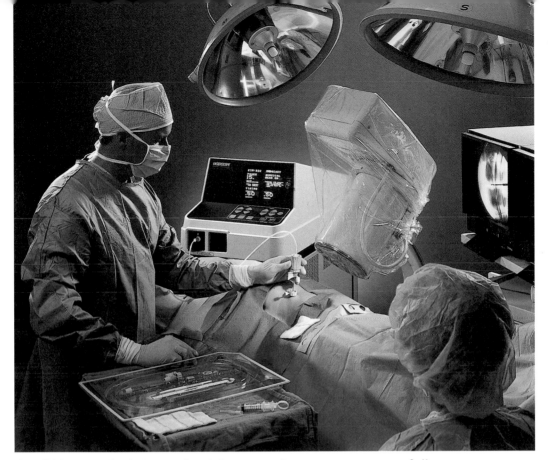

A KTP laser, which is made with potassium, uses very carefully targeted radiation to remove tattoos and other blemishes in the skin. The powerful energy of the laser can be controlled so closely that only a few cells in the outer layers are affected.

KTP laser gives off are absorbed by specific tissues that become hot. The heat destroys the targeted cells. Tattoos can be removed from the skin. Spider veins (the tiny, spreading veins that often show up in older people's legs) can be stopped and eliminated. Very delicate eye surgery can also be performed.

Sleep and Boredom

Potassium bromide, KBr, was once the main sedative used to calm people down and put them to sleep. It was called "taking a bromide." Perhaps because taking bromide medicines made people dull and boring, an idea that was dull and boring came to be called a bromide. (Bromine is Br, element #35.)

Working with Gold

Potassium plays several roles in working with gold (Au, element #79). Gold can be separated from ore that doesn't contain much of the valuable metal by using the chemical potassium cyanide, KCN. The low-grade ore is ground up and KCN is mixed in. The gold separates from the rest of the rock as a gold cyanide solution. Another chemical is added to make the gold separate out as a solid material called a precipitate. The solid is then treated with another chemical that releases the gold.

In a cyanide leaching pond, gold is separated from low-grade ore by chemical reaction with potassium cyanide. This process is very harmful to the environment.

Many environmentalists oppose the use of cyanides by mining companies to obtain gold. Cyanide, CN^-, is an ion that can get into the environment and kill plants and animals.

Statues and Olympic medals can be made to look gold by using the chemical gold potassium cyanide, $KAuCN_2$. The chemical is used as an electrolyte to apply a thin layer of gold to the item. This process is called electroplating. In a process similar to Humphry Davy's electrolysis, electricity splits the gold atoms away from the rest of the molecule. Gold atoms accumulate on the item being plated.

A Murder Mystery

A male nurse who worked at an Indiana hospital was found guilty in the 1990s of murdering six patients, though he may, over several years, have killed many, many more. An expert working with the police realized that the patients had all been in intensive care and had monitors recording their heart action. Their heart rhythms had all changed in a way that indicated they were getting far too much potassium. Later, the nurse was found to have a number of little bottles of potassium chloride, KCl, in his possession. The hardest part of the expert's job during the trail was making the jury understand just what role potassium plays in the beating of a human heart.

Making Great Medicines

Penicillin was the original antibiotic (a drug that kills bacteria). It was discovered by Scottish scientist Alexander Fleming in 1928. Penicillin is manufactured from a living mold that grows on another substance called the medium. Today, when it is being made, penicillin is isolated from the growing medium as a salt, often a potassium salt. Several forms of penicillin have potassium in them, such as penicillin V potassium, taken orally, and penicillin G potassium, which is given in injections.

A potassium chemical that was used for many decades to kill bacteria on skin was potassium permanganate, $KMnO_4$. Today, it is used primarily as an oxidant—it readily gives up its oxygen atoms to other materials. For example, when added to paper pulp, the oxygen combines with colored impurities, leaving a whiter product. Interestingly, this purple chemical is manufactured from potassium manganate, which is dark green in color.

Breathing Color

Color plays a great role in potassium reactions. One of these is in breathalyzer tests that police officers give to drivers if they think the drivers have had too much alcohol to drink. The driver breathes into a device that measures an exact amount of exhaled air. The air passes through orange-colored crystals, which are potassium dichromate, $K_2Cr_2O_7$. The alcohol content of the breath changes the dichromate to chromate. The chemical changes color in an exact relationship to the amount of alcohol in the driver's blood.

A policeman gives a driver a breathalyzer test that uses potassium compounds to show how much alcohol he has drunk.

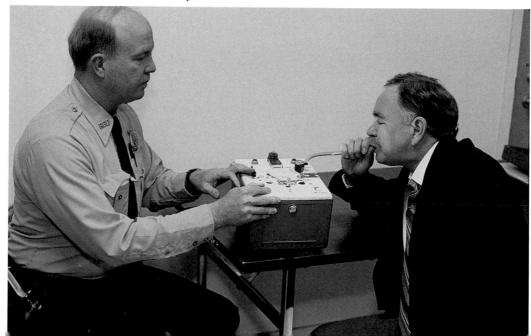

Stronger Bread

Bread dough made in commercial bakeries is sometimes strengthened by adding the chemical potassium bromate. However, scientists have known since 1982 that this compound can cause tumors of the kidney, thyroid, and other organs in animals. The United Kingdom and Canada have banned the use of potassium bromate in bread, but the United States has tried to get bakers voluntarily to stop using the chemical. The bakers who still use it say that the compound changes into a harmless substance during baking.

Baking up Crystals

A crystalline chemical known as Rochelle salt (chemically sodium potassium tartrate tetrahydrate) has many different uses, from serving as an additive to food to manufacturing the electronic components called semiconductors. These crystals can be manufactured from items found in a grocery store—baking soda and cream of tartar.

Baking soda is sodium bicarbonate, $NaHCO_3$. It is used both for heartburn (as is the similar potassium bicarbonate, $KHCO_3$) and to make baked goods lighter. When mixed with moist ingredients, it gives off carbon dioxide, which forms tiny bubbles in the dough, making it lighter and fluffier.

Cream of tartar, another potassium compound, is also used in cooking. Slightly acidic, it was originally manufactured from the materials left after wine was made. Today it is manufactured from tartaric acid and called potassium bitartrate. It is sometimes added to baking powder to help make dough rise.

In the year 2000, a national crystal-growing competition was held in Canadian high schools in recognition of National Chemistry Week. The competitors had to see how big a Rochelle crystal they could grow from grocery-store ingredients.

Potassium in Brief

Name: potassium, from the word *potash*

Symbol: K, for the Arabic *kalium,* meaning "potash"

Isolated by: Humphry Davy in 1807

Atomic number: 19

Atomic weight: 39.0983

Electrons in shells: 2, 8, 8, 1

Group: 1 (also called IA); other elements in Group 1 include lithium, sodium, rubidium, cesium, and francium

Usual characteristics: very soft silvery metal

Density (mass per unit volume): 0.86 g/cm³

Melting point (freezing point): 63.28° C (145.90° F)

Boiling point (liquefaction point): 760° C (1400° F)

Abundance:

  Earth: 7th most abundant element

  Earth's crust: 8th most abundant element

  Earth's atmosphere: None

  Ocean: 5th most abundant element

  Human body: 5th most abundant element

Stable isotopes (potassium atoms with different numbers of neutrons in their nuclei): two stable isotopes occur in nature: K-39, which is the most abundant (93.3% in rock), and K-41

Radioactive isotopes: K-40 occurs naturally; there are numerous artificial radioactive isotopes

Glossary

acid: definitions vary, but basically it is a corrosive substance that gives up a positive hydrogen ion (H+), equal to a proton when dissolved in water; indicates less than 7 on the pH scale because of its large number of hydrogen ions

alchemy: the combination of science, religion, and magic that preceded chemistry

alkali: a substance, such as an hydroxide or carbonate of an alkali metal, that when dissolved in water causes an increase in the hydroxide ion (OH-) concentration, forming a basic solution.

anion: an ion with a negative charge

atom: the smallest amount of an element that exhibits the properties of the element, consisting of protons, electrons, and (usually) neutrons

base: a substance that accepts a hydrogen ion (H+) when dissolved in water; indicates higher than 7 on the pH scale because of its small number of hydrogen ions

boiling point: the temperature at which a liquid at normal pressure evaporates into a gas, or a solid changes directly (sublimes) into a gas

bond: the attractive force linking atoms together in a molecule or crystal

catalyst: a substance that causes or speeds a chemical reaction without itself being consumed in the reaction

cation: an ion with a positive charge

chemical reaction: a transformation or change in a substance involving the electrons of the chemical elements making up the substance

combustion: burning, or rapid combination of a substance with oxygen, usually producing heat and light

compound: a substance formed by two or more chemical elements bound together by chemical means

crystal: a solid substance in which the atoms are arranged in three-dimensional patterns that create smooth outer surfaces, or faces

decompose: to break down a substance into its components

density: the amount of material in a given volume, or space; mass per unit volume; often stated as grams per cubic centimeter (g/cm^3)

diatomic: made up of two atoms

dissolve: to spread evenly throughout the volume of another substance

electrode: a device such as a metal plate that conducts electrons into or out of a solution or battery

electrolysis: the decomposition of a substance by electricity

electrolyte: a substance that conducts electricity when dissolved in water or when liquefied

element: a substance that cannot be split chemically into simpler substances that maintain the same characteristics. Each of the 103 naturally occurring chemical elements is made up of atoms of the same kind.

enzyme: one of the many complex proteins that act as biological catalysts in the body

evaporate: to change from a liquid to a gas

gas: a state of matter in which the atoms or molecules move freely, matching the shape and volume of the container holding it

group: a vertical column in the Periodic Table, with each element having similar physical and chemical characteristics; also called chemical family

half-life: the period of time required for half of a radioactive element to decay

hormone: any of various secretions of the endocrine glands that control different functions of the body, especially at the cellular level

inorganic: not containing carbon

ion: an atom or molecule that has acquired an electric charge by gaining or losing one or more electrons

ionic bond: a link between two atoms made by one atom taking one or more electrons from the other, giving the two atoms opposite electrical charges, which holds them together

isotope: an atom with a different number of neutrons in its nucleus from other atoms of the same element

mass number: the total of protons and neutrons in the nucleus of an atom

melting point: the temperature at which a solid becomes a liquid

metal: a chemical element that conducts electricity, usually shines, or reflects light, is dense, and can be shaped. About three-quarters of the naturally occurring elements are metals However, not all metals are elements.

metalloid: a chemical element that has some characteristics of a metal and some of a nonmetal; includes some elements in Groups 13 through 17 in the Periodic Table

molecule: the smallest amount of a substance that has the characteristics of the substance and usually consists of two or more atoms

neutral: 1) having neither acidic nor basic properties; 2) having no electrical charge

neutron: a subatomic particle within the nucleus of all atoms except hydrogen; has no electric charge

nonmetal: a chemical element that does not conduct electricity, is not dense, and is too brittle to be worked. Nonmetals easily form ions, and they include some elements in Groups 14 through 17 and all of Group 18 in the Periodic Table.

nucleus: 1) the central part of an atom, which has a positive electrical charge from its one or more protons; the nuclei of all atoms except hydrogen also include electrically neutral neutrons; 2) the central portion of most living cells, which controls the activities of the cells and contains the genetic material

organic: containing carbon

oxidation: the loss of electrons during a chemical reaction; need not necessarily involve the element oxygen

pH: an indicator of the acidity of a substance, on a scale of 0 to 14, with 7 being neutral. pH stands for "potential of hydrogen."

photosynthesis: in green plants, the process by which carbon dioxide and water, in the presence of light, are turned into sugars

pressure: the force exerted by an object divided by the area over which the force is exerted. The air at sea level exerts a pressure, called atmospheric pressure, of 14.7 pounds per square inch (1013 millibars).

protein: a complex biological chemical made by the linking of many amino acids

proton: a subatomic particle within the nucleus of all atoms; has a positive electric charge

radioactive: of an atom, spontaneously emitting high-energy particles

reduction: the gain of electrons, which occurs in conjunction with oxidation

respiration: the process of taking in oxygen and giving off carbon dioxide

salt: any compound that, with water, results from the neutralization of an acid by a base. In common usage, sodium chloride (table salt)

shell: a region surrounding the nucleus of an atom in which one or more electrons can occur. The inner shell can hold a maximum of two electrons; others may hold eight or more. If an atom's outer, or valence, shell does not hold its maximum number of electrons, the atom is subject to chemical reactions.

solid: a state of matter in which the shape of the collection of atoms or molecules does not depend on the container

solution: a mixture in which one substance is evenly distributed throughout another

synthetic: created in a laboratory instead of occurring naturally

valence electron: an electron located in the outer shell of an atom, available to participate in chemical reactions

vitamin: any of several organic substances, usually obtainable from a balanced diet, that the human body needs for specific physiological processes to take place

For Further Information

BOOKS

Atkins, P. W. *The Periodic Kingdom: A Journey into the Land of the Chemical Elements.* NY: Basic Books, 1995

Heiserman, David L. *Exploring Chemical Elements and Their Compounds,* Blue Ridge Summit, PA: Tab Books, 1992

Hoffman, Roald, and Vivian Torrence. *Chemistry Imagined: Reflections on Science.* Washington, DC: Smithsonian Institution Press, 1993

Newton, David E. *Chemical Elements.* Venture Books. Danbury, CT: Franklin Watts, 1994

Yount, Lisa. *Antoine Lavoisier: Founder of Modern Chemistry.* "Great Minds of Science" series. Springfield, NJ: Enslow Publishers, 1997

Newton, David E. *Chemical Elements: From Carbon to Krypton.* 3 volumes. Detroit: UXL, 1998

CD-ROM

Discover the Elements: The Interactive Periodic Table of the Chemical Elements, Paradigm Interactive, Greensboro, NC, 1995

INTERNET SITES

Note that useful sites on the Internet can change and even disappear. If the following site addresses do not work, use a search engine that you find useful, such as: Yahoo:

> http://www.yahoo.com

or Google:

> http://google.com

or Encyclopaedia Britannica:

> http://britannica.com

A very thorough listing of the major characteristics, uses, and compounds of all the chemical elements can be found at a site called WebElements:

> http://www.web-elements.com

Many subjects are covered on WWW Virtual Library. It also includes a useful collection of links to other sites:

> http://www.earthsystems.org/Environment/shtml

Index

11-01